Journey

Sue Lewis

Cinnamon Press
:: small miracles from distinctive voices ::

Published by Cinnamon Press
Office 49019, PO Box 92, Cardiff, CF11 1NB.
www.cinnamonpress.com

ISBN 978-1-78864-132-6

British Library Cataloguing in Publication Data. A CIP record for this book can be obtained from the British Library.

Designed and typeset in Bodoni by Cinnamon Press. Cover design by Adam Craig.

Cinnamon Press is represented by Inpress Ltd.

Acknowledgements

With much gratitude to Jan Fortune for sharing her craft and for the unique poetic focus of Cinnamon Press.

Thanks also to Croydon's Poets Anonymous for keeping me sane through the pandemic lockdowns; to Vicky and Tony at the Chi Clinic who kept the chi flowing; to Peter for the gift of music and to Sara for her inadvertent inspiration.

And thank you also to David, to my sister Helen and to Kathryn and James, my bright stars.

Contents

For Stella (1930-2021)

Journey

The way it is

This is the way it is.
Rain, falling on a velvet night;
moon wrapped in a shroud.
The sky poured out on
trees and empty streets:
tonight there seems no end to it.
Murmured water scatters,
soft and spitting, at the glass:
on and on, a punctuated prophecy.
Something is about to happen:
some feat of transubstantiation,
crimson ripe astringency about to burst.
I cannot walk beyond the mirror;
penetrate the labyrinth of the past.
But neither can I peel the layers
of this fragile leaf apart.
For everything is intricately joined.
You are the flip side of my coin:
that same currency involved.
The rain falls on and on
and there's no sleep.
For this is how things are.

Journey

Useful directions, so you tell me,
depend upon the starting point.

I must begin again.

Each turning that we take
depends on so much else:

how choices race towards us
while we're all mis-reading maps;
how precious things
get left behind.

How soon the soft young
green of summer withers;
how the rain mists up the view.

How, when you drive out
from the centre of a starry sky,
you hold your breath against
the cold of winter coming.

And how the cat's-eye of a
crescent moon, carved radish-thin,
will sometimes serve to light you
when you lose your way.

Go back and start again.
Take nothing with you
but the burden of your loving.
Carry it with care and, this time,
do not put it down.

Somewhat glorious

Like a flame, rekindled,
we must carry this in
careful hands; not crush it.
Give it air and room.
Walk up underneath
the marvellous light of it.
Suffer its sweet burn.

None of us could
see this coming:
didn't hear its arrow-rush.
Just felt the splinter of it
as it worked itself in deep.
And all of us were torn
and some will not come back.

In time, let us resume our
somewhat glorious life;
our tapestry of shimmer,
woven from the snipped-off threads.
Who has another chance like we do?
We must wrap ourselves
within its texture; put it on parade.
Return it, undiminished, to the earth.

How beautiful it is. How fragile.

Transmuted

You text me at my deepest hour:
flint-winter purity of falling light.
A stained-glass window catches fire:
magenta, topaz, indigo.

I read, re-read your invitation
like an opening chord. Praeludium.
And I am salvaged by your perfect pitch,
your precise beat. Your slant of sun.

You are my consolation,
turning up the way you have,
riddling out this burnt and blackened year
and I can't ask for more.

Spring will come, I know that now.
The white magnolias.

Evasion

Leave the thing unsaid;
that way it can't be used against you.
Leave the thing unsaid but
do not blame me if it
comes at you some other way.

Don't blame me if the evening
wraps its scarlet round you
and your music flames to gold;
if shadows ebonise your garden
and your dreams are tinted indigo.

Leave the thing unsaid: it will
insist throughout your midnight hours.
Mute, you'll find that sleep won't come.
Unsaid things can never stay unspoken;
stopped words are deft at cutting through.

Dew on the grass: new page of morning
opens to the scent of mint, of lavender.
Immoderate fragrance of tomato leaves.
Don't blame me when the thing unspoken
speaks itself some other way.

Marginalia

Old book. You open
at a page we both agree upon.
Put on a shelf a long time past;
and left for dead.
But here you are:
your cover showing signs of age
though everything is there.
And more: those pencilled words,
those underlinings, exclamation marks.
I comb your margins, carefully,
to see if I can find myself.

Evergreen

Ghost in your own garden,
falling down between the cracks.
Close-wrapped, tight-staked,
shut in for winter. Yet you
dream of freedom blazing,
unmasked vibrant summer gold.
Of scratching at the tilth
with ungloved hands,
of standing out in rain;
not coming in till dusk.

These are small things to crave.
You're sorting seeds at midnight:
powerful amulets against the dark.

Invocation

That empty afternoon at Delphi,
bright Apollo came to meet me
in a cloud of light, disguised.
A golden dog who tracked me
from the sacred temenos
down sun-fired paths through
chamomile and thyme.

So quiet, all I could hear was
far-off flocks across the valley,
bells tolling at their sacrificial necks.
For nothing changes, after all:
why would the old gods not be there?
So, Aphrodite, you will hear my prayer.
But, fickle, you may laugh at me.

Astraeus

Dusk. The sun spreads out its honey on the far hill, soaks like sherry into sponge cake; disappears. Daytime certainties begin to blur; soft shadows shuffle closer, start their adorations. Birds fall silent and the trees stand quiet as horses, in a circle, night almost upon them. He owns this time now: breathes its subtle fade. Its liminal, embodied wait. He feels it like a broken arrow which he can't draw out; his burden and his birth right. His thoughts are owl wings, silently aligned and spread: one ear listening to the ground, quartering the dry, late-summer field, picking up the tiny murmurs, possibilities; rustles boxed within the long, bleached grass. The other concentrating on the hymn of sky; thin sounds from above. He is quivering; feathered with intent. The dark slips softly round his head, across his body: he enters it like water, lets it flow across him. The doors are open to the evening; soon he'll slip outside, welcome the air, the hot flame of the day now dissipated, cooling. Bats hunt here above the stream: tiny triangles of ragged silk which susurrate between the trees and out across the water. But they respect him: they won't bother him. He's waiting on the stars. His stars. Yearns for their light. Their strigine silver. He is quiet, quiet. And wise. Now in his solemn, serious face, there is the haunt of longing. Obscure velvet in the blood. His hair has that spangled, lustrous, evening sheen. He cloaks himself. For it is time. Watchful of him at first, and then more proudly, his beloved winds begin to blow.

Fog

Listen to
the silence
thick as sleep.

The lovely fields
are painted out.

The world has closed
to just this room:
no sound, no sight.

No clocks here
marking off the hours,
no post, no telephone.

Outside,
the canvas chairs are sodden
and the grass is wet.

No morning blackbird
and my words, unsaid.

Solvitur ambulando

Later, I will walk my old bronze river:
hear it slopping, sucking at the bank.
Stand beneath the sail of morning:
nets of lifting mist, backlit by sun.

Memories are scattered ashes;
life's brief flaring, scythed and burnt.
Brave weir: austere infinity of falling,
roaring, glassy, into murderous froth.

Smell the musk and rot of autumn:
unpicked brambles. Left to haunt.
Time here oozes, slithers backwards
through the tunnel of my thoughts.

Shell

You had a presence once.

But now your empty curve
weighs light inside my hand.

Bone-dry, annulled.

Although the music,
in your absence, still
                    connects us.

Howling in the blood.

Antiphonal

For a short while there
is only this: the water,
sky. Call and response.

I drop a pebble
into your serenity;
your gift of silence.

Paradoxical:
your omnipresent absence.
Ripples fanning out.

Second light

I get better. I have healed but
somehow I have shed a skin.
I find myself amazed, for everything
is new and every sound too loud.
A struck match deafens and the
washing-up is pitched too sharp.
I marvel at the way the light comes in:
at footsteps in the morning street,
the acid yellow of mahonia flowers,
blue dance of skyline, citrus frost upon the grass.
The colours brighter, louder:
something's shifted and it's NOW
and every second lasts for ever.
I have crossed into some rare dimension
where there is no sense of separation.
Bliss is what I feel:
complete and unconditional compassion.
Mine is a body of broken halves:
my mouth is full of chewed up paper
and the words come out all wrong.
My eyebrows ache. My hand, hawk-heavy,
fumbles with the scissors, knives.
Stand well back from the edge.
When I put my foot down,
sometimes there is nothing underneath.
Money is a puzzling currency.
But do not pity me:
I have never felt so nakedly alive.
Wisdom tells me that this will not last.
I cannot analyse. This will not come again:
this single pebble that I hold is borrowed
from a distant beach of sharp-lit solitude.
In time, I'll excavate the past for clues;
fall off the cliff-edge of the future.
Right now, the teacups are too loud.

Pomegranate

Everything now is
stained with hope,
the juice of possibility.
Ripe pomegranate blush.
New mornings open
while we hold our breath;
vermilion on our far horizon.
Even rain delights me now:
soft amber jazz percussion.
How do I live with all this
sudden brilliance?
I stay awake all night,
longing for the salt;
the everyday enchantment.

Muse

Stormy night and she turns up: she's always doing this.
The wind is drilling through my house; taking things apart.
Papers are a pigeon's nest: undrunk cups of tea perch on the desk.
She's damp and dripping on my hardwood floor;
her hair is soaked. She shivers. Wipes her chilled moon face.
I sit her down and light a fire.

She asks me what I'm writing now. I sketch out plans
for my slim book of angst. She shakes her head:
the snakes, thank god, are very still tonight.
Well, I say (I wish she'd go) it helps to write it out.
So much is missing: lost within the gaps.
A forked tongue flickers, briefly, by her ear.
She chews a Nicorette and folds her still-damp chiton
round her sodden Nikes: more Croydon than Olympos.
Why am I stuck with her?

Despair can be a bugger, don't I know, she sighs.
But listen: no-one wants to read about your boring life.
When I refuse outright to take her pills, she mentions Freud,
and Jung, Adler and Klein. And helps herself to wine.
The snakes are coming loose, their firelit eyes fixed on the cat…
I'll counsel you, she says. Let's see what will come out.
But have you any crisps? I'm ravenous.

Vellichor

Second-hand books
with Dewey marks:
wistful, overwintering birds.
Some gaunt, some shabby,
some with plumage missing,
some with broken spines.

They lean together for the warmth;
they smell of rainy afternoons.
On dusky nights, in husky voices,
some of them sing softly, a cappella.
All the old songs.

Sometimes, they bring cargo:
a letter or forgotten sketch.
A map, a faded photograph;
quixotic remnants of another time,
another place. Passed subtly on.

Kintsugi

Almost winter.

But the leaves are stubborn:
the gist of it seems wrong.
Birds are shrieking, flirting:
something's broken; out of true.
The sky's inscribed by senseless flight:
luke-warm and sullen as a bruise.

What's needed is the shock   of snow.

You hide your scars like I do:
we might not be beyond repair.
Let's keep the broken pieces safe,
close-wrapped in autumn.
One day we'll lay them out.
See what goes where.

Ellipsis

We left each other
on a beach somewhere;
fast-running down a busy street
or sitting in some crowded bar.
For always there's a
time for losing things:
the wrench of life gets in the way.
We grew our skilful wings
and learned to fly;
took different paths
out of the wood.
But, strangely, there's a
time for finding, too.
The flyways intersect; ripe
sanguine moon still lights us both.
Now, at the crossroads, we have
picked each other up again.
Held gently, in our outstretched hands,
are seeds. For our returning bird.

Postscript

In a box which
once held Spanish soap,
I find your letter
pressed between
old photographs;
some snips of baby hair;
my children's bargains
with the Tooth Fairy;
their Santa shopping lists.

Three pages, closely written;
lost words which resonate
a sense of you. Unique.
Some things can never change.

The heat today is off the scale:
the box still holds its perfume.

Lightning Source UK Ltd.
Milton Keynes UK
UKHW012216010222
398051UK00001B/79